RETURN TO YELLOWSTONE

GRAY WOLF COMEBACK

BY TIM COOKE

ILLUSTRATED BY EDU COLL

BEARPORT
PUBLISHING

Minneapolis, Minnesota

Credits: 20, © Holly Kuchera/Shutterstock; 21, © Holly Kuchera/Shutterstock; 22t, © Jean-Edouard Rozey/Shutterstock; 22b, © Henk Bogaard/Shutterstock.

Editor: Sarah Eason
Proofreader: Harriet McGregor
Designers: Jessica Moon and Steve Mead
Picture Researcher: Rachel Blount

DISCLAIMER: This graphic story is a dramatization based on true events. It is intended to give the reader a sense of the narrative rather than a presentation of actual details as they occurred.

Library of Congress Cataloging-in-Publication Data

Names: Cooke, Tim, 1961- author. | Coll, Edu, 1996- illustrator.
Title: Return to Yellowstone : gray wolf comeback / by Tim Cooke ;
   illustrated by Edu Coll.
Description: Bear claw books edition. | Minneapolis, Minnesota : Bearport
   Publishing Company, [2022] | Series: Saving animals from the brink |
   Includes bibliographical references and index.
Identifiers: LCCN 2020058601 (print) | LCCN 2020058602 (ebook) | ISBN
   9781636910468 (library binding) | ISBN 9781636910536 (paperback) | ISBN
   9781636910604 (ebook)
Subjects: LCSH: Leopold, Aldo, 1886-1948--Juvenile literature. | Gray
   wolf--Reintroduction--Yellowstone National Park--Juvenile literature. |
   Endangered species--Conservation--Yellowstone National Park--Juvenile
   literature.
Classification: LCC QL737.C22 C633 2022 (print) | LCC QL737.C22 (ebook) |
   DDC 599.77309787/52--dc23
LC record available at https://lccn.loc.gov/2020058601
LC ebook record available at https://lccn.loc.gov/2020058602

For more information, write to Bearport Publishing, 5357 Penn Avenue South, Minneapolis, MN 55419. Printed in the United States of America.

CONTENTS

CHAPTER 1

LAND OF THE WOLF

About 400 years ago, millions of wolves roamed the North American wilderness.

These **apex predators** were an important part of the land's **ecosystem**. They helped keep the numbers of different animals in balance.

But when European **settlers** arrived in the 1600s, life for the wolves began to change.

5

In the 1700s and 1800s, the wolf population steadily declined.

THE WOLVES ARE KILLING OUR COWS!

Many wolves were killed by farmers trying to protect their **livestock**.

Hunters also killed wolves to sell their **pelts**.

By the 1900s, nearly all the wolves in North America were gone.

In 1944, a scientist named Aldo Leopold had an idea to save the wolves from **extinction**. He suggested **reintroducing** the animals to Yellowstone National Park. But it would still be 50 years before his plan became reality.

CHAPTER 2

A BOLD PLAN

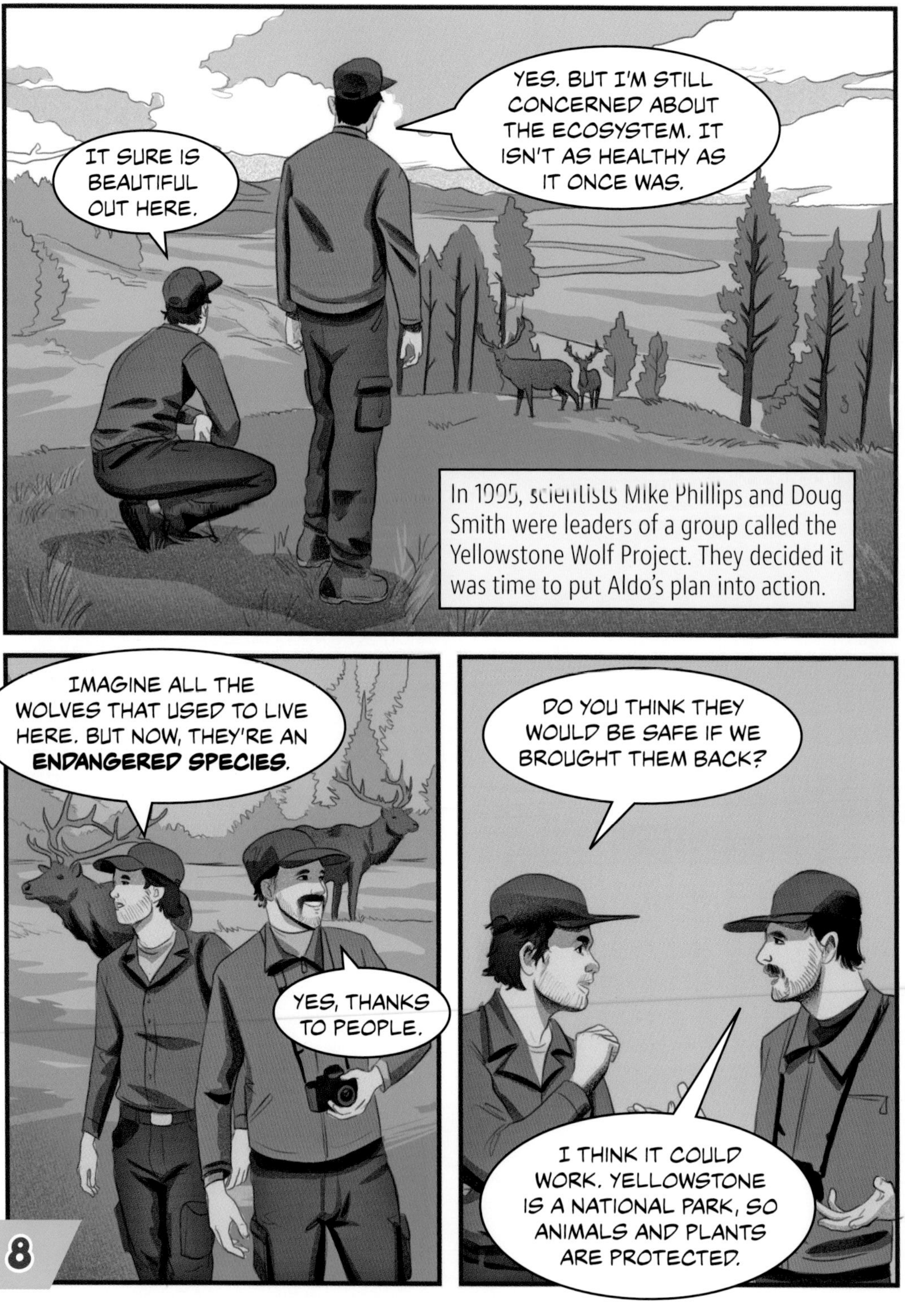
IT SURE IS BEAUTIFUL OUT HERE.
YES. BUT I'M STILL CONCERNED ABOUT THE ECOSYSTEM. IT ISN'T AS HEALTHY AS IT ONCE WAS.
In 1995, scientists Mike Phillips and Doug Smith were leaders of a group called the Yellowstone Wolf Project. They decided it was time to put Aldo's plan into action.
IMAGINE ALL THE WOLVES THAT USED TO LIVE HERE. BUT NOW, THEY'RE AN **ENDANGERED SPECIES**.
YES, THANKS TO PEOPLE.
DO YOU THINK THEY WOULD BE SAFE IF WE BROUGHT THEM BACK?
I THINK IT COULD WORK. YELLOWSTONE IS A NATIONAL PARK, SO ANIMALS AND PLANTS ARE PROTECTED.

Mike and Doug created a plan to **relocate** wolves from Canada.

LOOK—OVER THERE!

LET'S GO!

They worked with **biologists** to safely move the animals.

LATER, WE'LL BE ABLE TO TRACK THIS WOLF'S MOVEMENTS BY USING **SIGNALS** FROM A RADIO COLLAR.

Each wolf was fitted with a collar before being brought to Yellowstone.

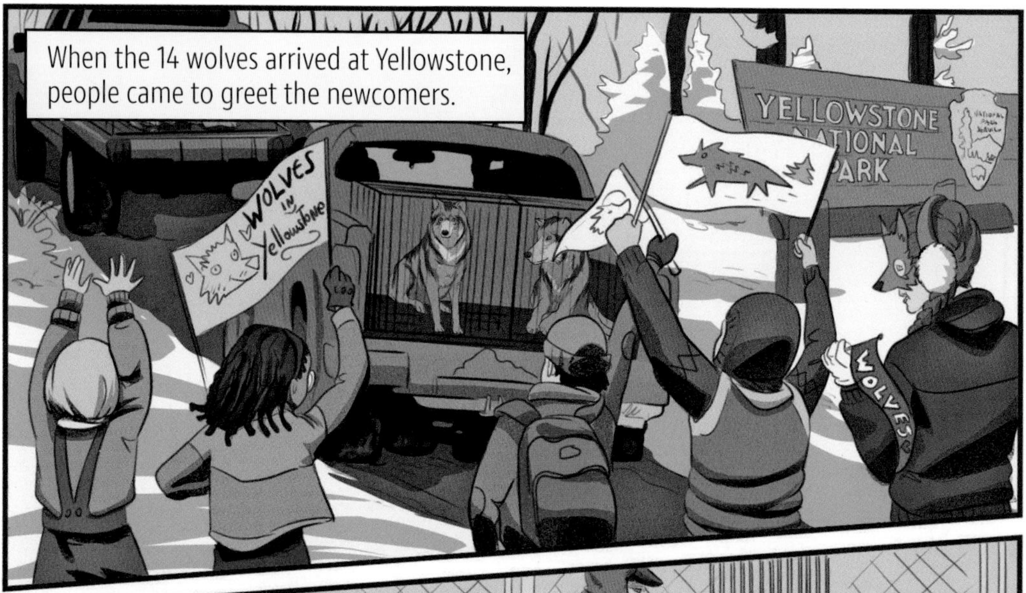
When the 14 wolves arrived at Yellowstone, people came to greet the newcomers.
WOLVES IN Yellowstone
YELLOWSTONE
WOLVES

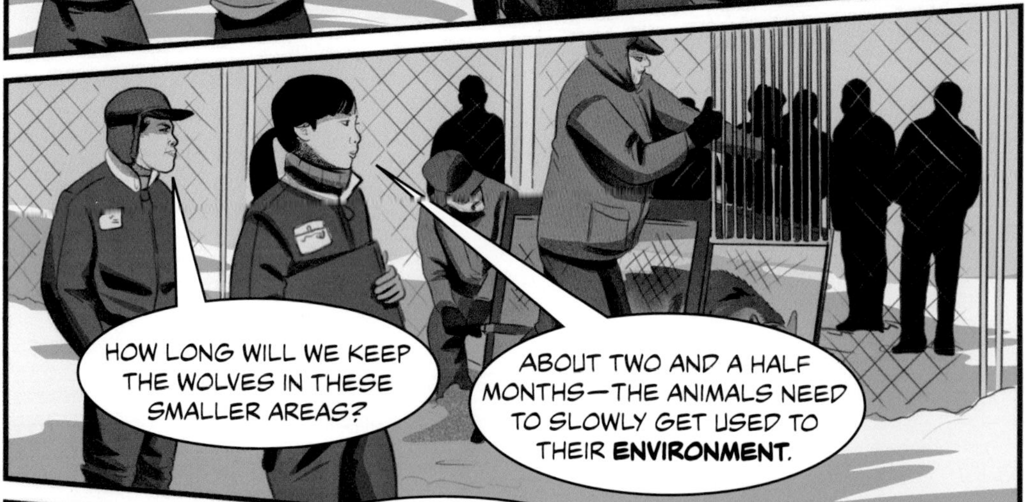
HOW LONG WILL WE KEEP THE WOLVES IN THESE SMALLER AREAS?
ABOUT TWO AND A HALF MONTHS—THE ANIMALS NEED TO SLOWLY GET USED TO THEIR **ENVIRONMENT**.

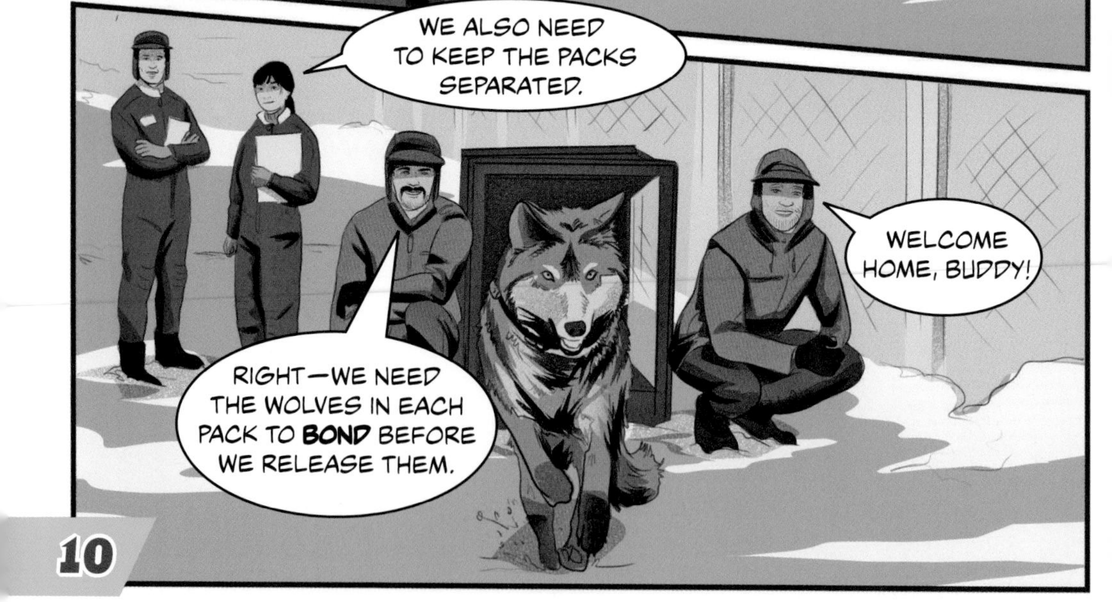
WE ALSO NEED TO KEEP THE PACKS SEPARATED.
WELCOME HOME, BUDDY!
RIGHT—WE NEED THE WOLVES IN EACH PACK TO **BOND** BEFORE WE RELEASE THEM.

After 10 weeks, the wolves were released into the full park.

For several weeks, Mike and Doug used the radio collars to track the wolves' movements in the park.

With hunters nearby, Mike and Doug knew any wolves that left Yellowstone would be in danger.

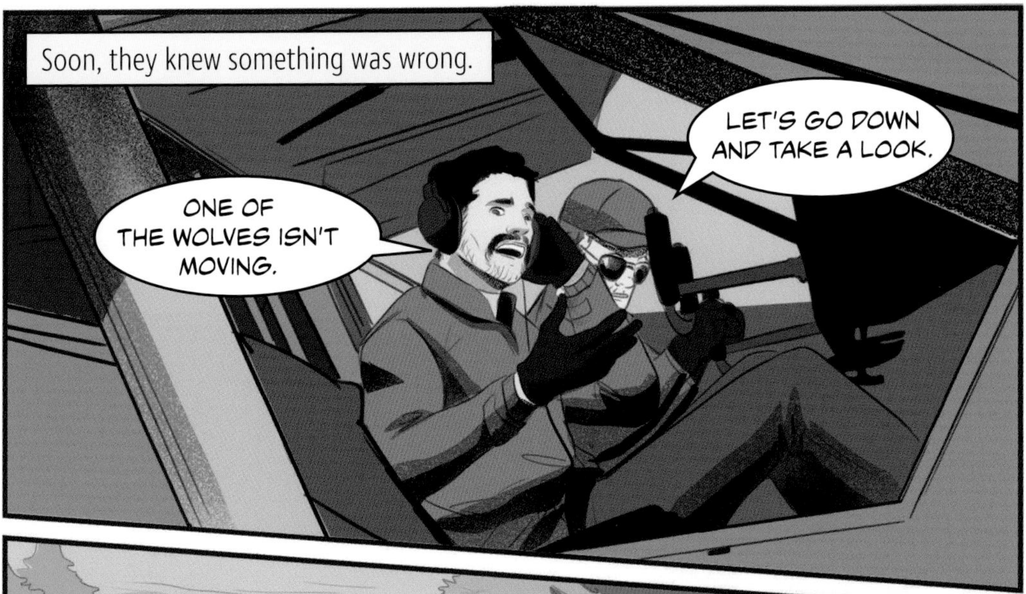
Soon, they knew something was wrong.
ONE OF THE WOLVES ISN'T MOVING.
LET'S GO DOWN AND TAKE A LOOK.

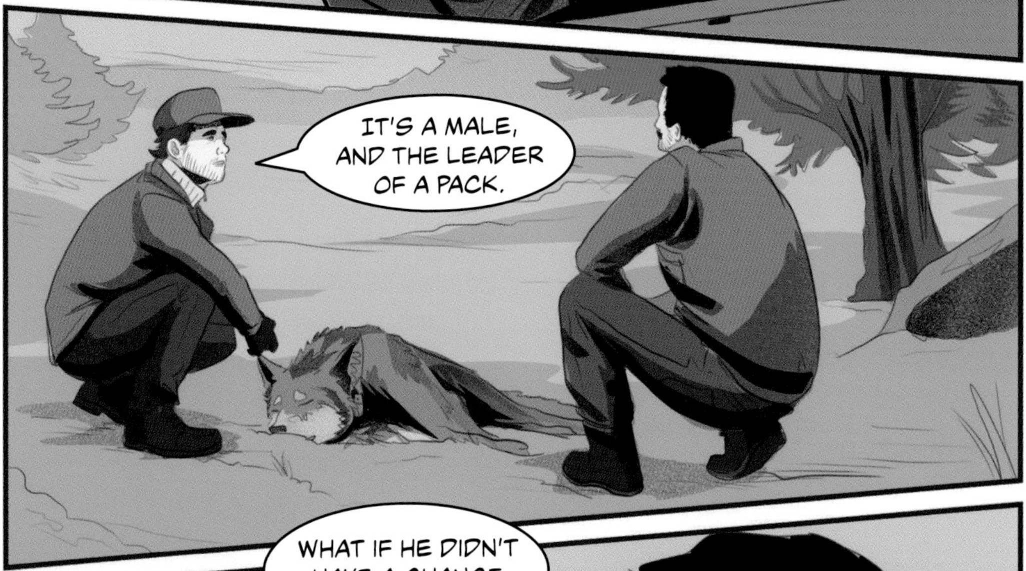
IT'S A MALE, AND THE LEADER OF A PACK.

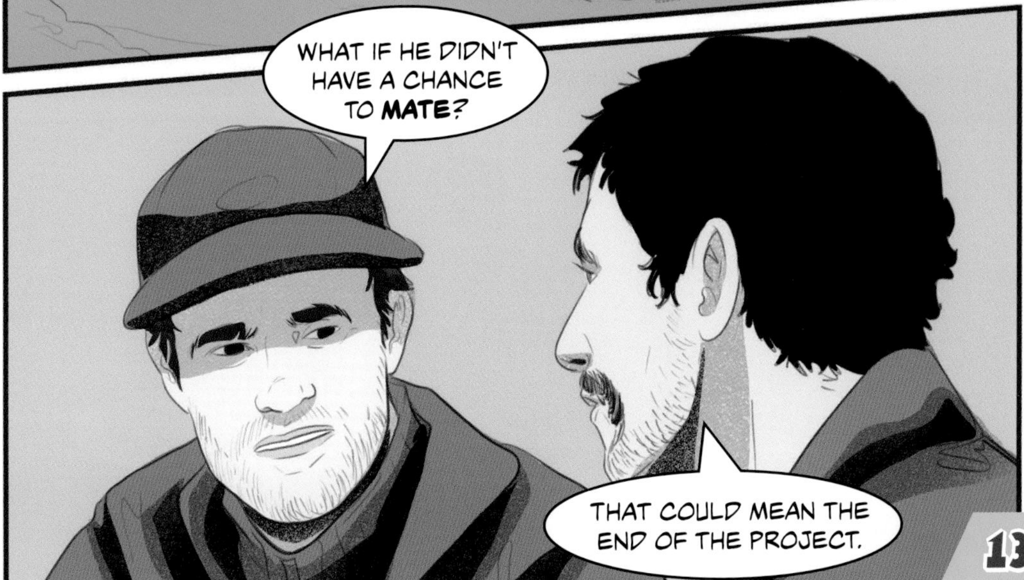
WHAT IF HE DIDN'T HAVE A CHANCE TO **MATE**?
THAT COULD MEAN THE END OF THE PROJECT.

CHAPTER 3

PROTECT THE WOLVES

Luckily, a **litter** of wolf pups was found a few weeks later.

WHAT CUTE PUPS!

AND THEY ALL LOOK HEALTHY.

A year later, more wolves were brought to Yellowstone to help increase the population.

SEVENTEEN NEW WOLVES! LET'S HOPE THEY SETTLE IN AS WELL AS THE FIRST GROUP.

THE PUPS FROM THE FIRST GROUP ARE ALREADY ADULTS.

Soon, the whole park's ecosystem began to improve.

IT LOOKS LIKE THE PLANTS AND ANIMALS HERE ARE GETTING STRONGER.

AND IT'S ALL THANKS TO THE WOLVES.

The wolves hunted elk. What they didn't eat themselves became food for eagles, ravens, and other animals.

With fewer elk eating the plants, there were soon more trees in the park. More trees meant that more birds had a place to live and more beavers could build dams.

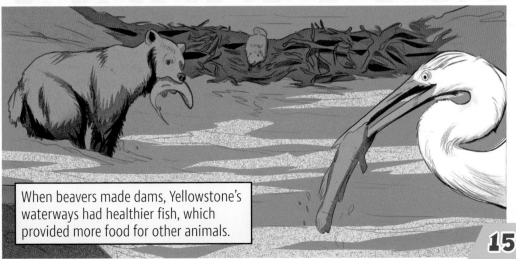

When beavers made dams, Yellowstone's waterways had healthier fish, which provided more food for other animals.

Some people were still unhappy about the wolves' return. Nearby farmers were concerned about their livestock.

THOSE WOLVES ARE BACK AGAIN.

A program was set up to pay farmers who lost livestock to wolves. At last, wolves could live safely in Yellowstone.

17

The wolf population steadily grew.

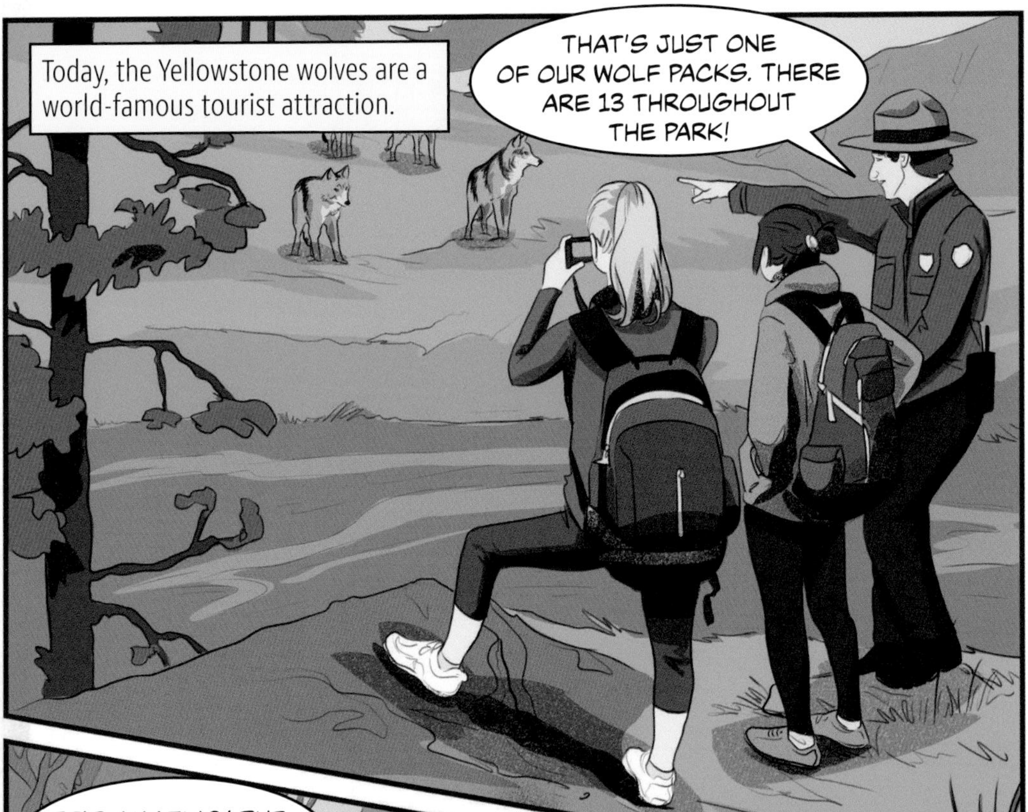
Today, the Yellowstone wolves are a world-famous tourist attraction.
THAT'S JUST ONE OF OUR WOLF PACKS. THERE ARE 13 THROUGHOUT THE PARK!

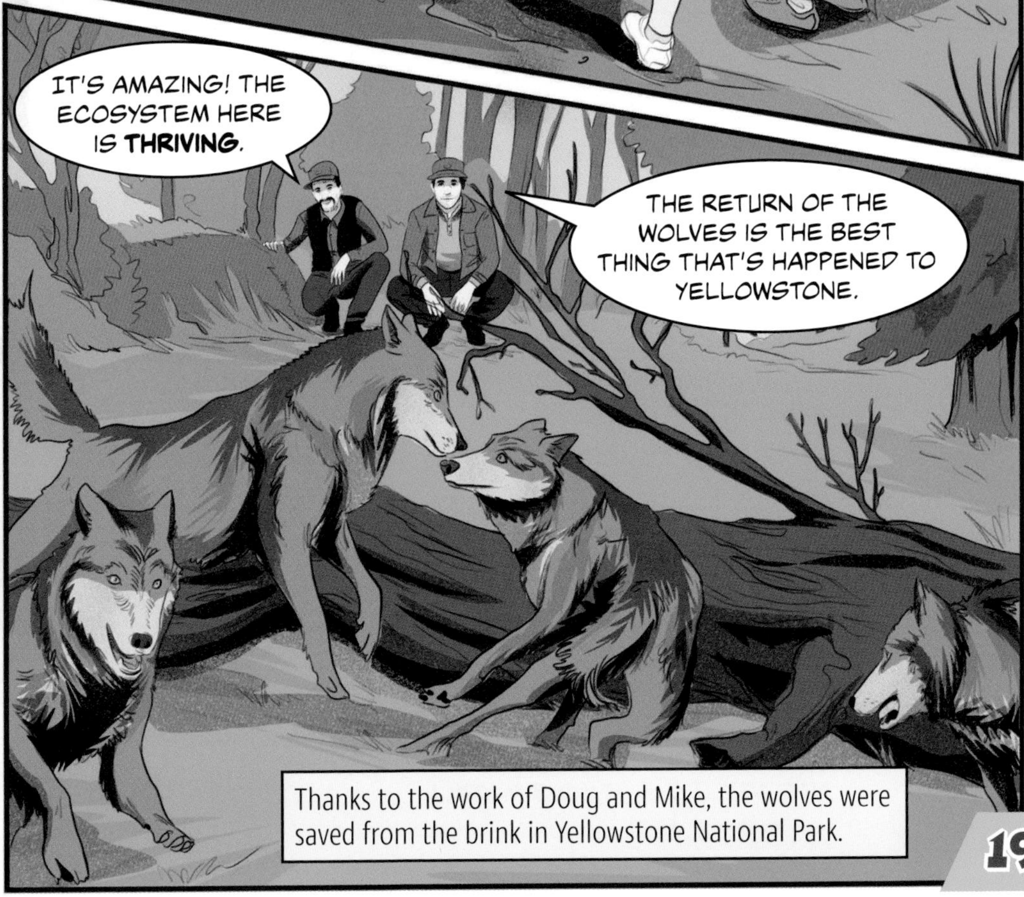
IT'S AMAZING! THE ECOSYSTEM HERE IS **THRIVING**.
THE RETURN OF THE WOLVES IS THE BEST THING THAT'S HAPPENED TO YELLOWSTONE.
Thanks to the work of Doug and Mike, the wolves were saved from the brink in Yellowstone National Park.

GRAY WOLF FACTS

In 1973, Congress passed the Endangered Species Act. This law protects animals and plants that are in danger of dying out in the United States. Harmful activities, such as hunting, capturing, or collecting endangered species, are **illegal** under this act.

GRAY WOLVES MEASURE 5-6.5 FEET (1.5-2 M) FROM NOSE TO TAIL. THEY ARE ABOUT 2.5 FT (0.8 M) TALL.

GRAY WOLVES EAT MOOSE, ELK, AND DEER.

The gray wolf was one of the first animals listed under the Endangered Species Act. This protection has helped bring the wolf population back.

In 1600, there were approximately two million wolves in North America. Now, that number is closer to 78,000.

OTHER WOLVES IN DANGER

The gray wolves at Yellowstone are one kind of wolf that's making a comeback. However, other types of wolves are still struggling.

RED WOLF

There are fewer than a dozen known wild red wolves in the world today. They are highly endangered. Red wolves were once found across the southeastern United States, from Texas to Florida, and north to the Carolinas, Kentucky, Illinois, and Missouri. They need to be saved from the brink.

RED WOLVES HAVE BEEN REINTRODUCED IN NORTH CAROLINA.

THERE ARE ONLY AROUND 500 WILD ETHIOPIAN WOLVES IN THE WORLD.

ETHIOPIAN WOLF

Ethiopian wolves are sometimes called Abyssinian wolves. They live in a country in northeastern Africa called Ethiopia. Half of all Ethiopian wolves live in Bale Mountains National Park in southern Ethiopia. It is illegal to hunt them.

GLOSSARY

apex predators animals that are not killed by any other animals

biologists scientists who study plants or animals

bond to form a close relationship

ecosystem a community of animals and plants that depend on one another to live

endangered species a group of animals in danger of dying out

environment the area where an animal lives

extinction to completely die out

illegal against the law

litter baby animals born to a mother at the same time

livestock farm animals

mate to come together to produce young

pelts animal skins with fur

reintroducing bringing an animal back to a place where the same animals once lived

relocate to move something to another area

settlers people who made a home and lived in a new place

signals communications given off by a radio

thriving doing very well

INDEX

READ MORE

Herrington, Lisa M. *Gray Wolves (Nature's Children)*. New York: Children's Press, 2018.

O'Brien, Cynthia. *Bringing Back the Gray Wolf (Animals Back from the Brink)*. New York: Crabtree Publishing, 2019.

Sommer, Nathan. *Grizzly Bear vs. Wolf Pack (Animal Battles)*. Minneapolis: Bellwether Media, 2020.

LEARN MORE ONLINE

1. Go to **www.factsurfer.com**

2. Enter "**Wolf Comeback**" into the search box.

3. Click on the cover of this book to see a list of websites.